ALBATROSSES

P9-EDD-449

First published in Great Britain in 2011 by
Colin Baxter Photography Ltd., Grantown-on-Spey, Moray, PH26 3TA, Scotland

www.colinbaxter.co.uk

Text copyright © 2011 Tony Martin
All rights reserved.

No part of this book may be reproduced, stored in a retrieval system or transmitted in any
form or by any means without the prior written permission of the publishers.

Map on pages 68-69 courtesy of the Global Procellariiform Tracking Database and BirdLife International.
Maps on page 70 courtesy of British Antarctic Survey.

WorldLife Library Series

A CIP Catalogue record for this book is available from the British Library.
ISBN 978-1-84107-403-0

Photography copyright © 2011 by:

Front cover © Colin Baxter
Back cover © Colin Baxter
Page 1 © Frans Lanting/lanting.com
Page 3 © Frans Lanting/lanting.com
Page 4 © Chris Gomersall/naturepl.com
Page 6 © Chris Gomersall/naturepl.com
Page 8 © Colin Baxter
Page 10 © Tony Martin
Page 12 © Colin Baxter
Page 13 © Claudio Contreras/naturepl.com
Page 15 © Doug Allan/naturepl.com
Page 16 © Mike Potts/naturepl.com
Page 19 © Frans Lanting/lanting.com
Page 20 © Colin Baxter
Page 21 © David Tipling/naturepl.com
Page 22 © Frans Lanting/lanting.com
Page 24 © Tony Martin
Page 25 © Solvin Zankl/naturepl.com
Page 26 © Terry Andrewartha/naturepl.com
Page 27 © Colin Baxter
Page 29 © Tony Martin
Page 30 © Frans Lanting/lanting.com
Page 33 © Frans Lanting/lanting.com

Page 34 © Pete Oxford/naturepl.com
Page 37 © Aleks Terauds
Page 39 © Colin Baxter
Page 40 © Tony Martin
Page 41 © Aleks Terauds
Page 42 © Aleks Terauds
Page 43 © Aleks Terauds
Page 44 © Eric Baccega/naturepl.com
Page 45 © Aleks Terauds
Page 46 © Tony Martin
Page 48 © Colin Baxter
Page 50 © Frans Lanting/lanting.com
Page 53 © Colin Baxter
Page 54 © Mike Potts/naturepl.com
Page 55 © Tony Martin
Page 56 © Aflo/naturepl.com
Page 57 © Frans Lanting/lanting.com
Page 58 © Peter Reese/naturepl.com
Page 59 © Colin Baxter
Page 60 © Pete Oxford/naturepl.com
Page 63 © Aleks Terauds
Page 64 © Frans Lanting/lanting.com
Page 67 © Frans Lanting/lanting.com

Printed in China.

ALBATROSSES

Tony Martin

Colin Baxter Photography, Grantown-on-Spey, Scotland

With complements from CHEESEMANS' ECOLOGY SAFARIS

Contents

Foreword by Dame Ellen MacArthur

It was a huge privilege for me to have been accompanied by graceful albatrosses while under sail in the Southern Ocean, and subsequently to have spent time with them at their breeding colonies on South Georgia. Watching them effortlessly glide over the water is quite mesmerising, and for me they have a spiritual presence.

Not only are these graceful oceanic wanderers extraordinary in flight, but I discovered that they lead truly extraordinary lives. They mate for life, can live into their 60s, may have just one chick every two years, and can circle the world in 46 days, returning to exactly the same spot without any navigational equipment! But the fact that bowled me over was that the young, once they leave the nest, will not return to land for between three and seven years. Now that's incredible in my opinion, and when you watch them land you realise that not a lot of landing practice is done!

Recently, I was fortunate enough to join a fantastic team of researchers carrying out work on albatrosses and petrels around South Georgia. On that journey was the author of this book, Tony Martin, and for weeks we travelled up and down the coast of this magical island, monitoring their numbers and meeting albatrosses face-to-face. This was a life-changing experience for me. It is staggering at times how humankind can be so blindly destructive on its mission for survival. The accidental capture of albatrosses on the hooks of longline fishing boats is placing all but a few of the 24 species of albatross in danger of extinction. Mitigation measures to solve this are simple and effective, and extremely low-cost, so why are albatrosses still dying in their thousands every year?

It is very real when you go there and speak to the scientists. When you find the hooks beside the nests on these remote islands – hooks which have been swallowed by adult albatrosses in fish heads, fed to their young and miraculously have not killed these lucky few – you realise how man's impact reaches to the ends of the earth.

It is down to us to make the changes necessary to stop this catastrophic killing of the innocent, because sadly most hooked albatrosses do not live to learn their lesson. I would love to think that these ocean friends will continue to grace us with their presence at sea for thousands of years to come.

Albatrosses

'I now belong to a higher cult of favored mortals, for I have seen the albatross!'
Robert Cushman Murphy (Field notes, October 28th 1912)

Unlike Murphy, a distinguished ornithologist from the American Museum of Natural History, most people reading these words have never been fortunate enough to see a live albatross, yet are motivated to open a book about a creature that may live half a world away. There is something about albatrosses that captivates the human imagination in a way that few other birds do. Perhaps it's their elegance and beauty, perhaps their complete mastery of the air, or their seemingly effortless ability to cross vast oceans. Perhaps it's because they are to us the quintessential embodiment of freedom — freedom to travel wherever they want, when they want. Or perhaps it is because of their mystery, which has for centuries held seafarers in awe and wonderment, and has resulted in mythology and folklore unrivalled by any other creature of the air. In the following pages we will explore the reality of the albatross world, and see that this bird needs neither myth nor exaggeration to inspire and entrance us, even as some of its mystery is peeled away by exciting new research and discovery.

Albatrosses are famously birds of the open ocean, coming to land only to breed, and the majority live in the middle and high latitudes of the Southern Hemisphere — further south than all the major centres of human population around the world. Unless you happen to live in Hawaii, southern New Zealand, Tasmania or the Falkland Islands, it is unlikely that you will see an albatross near home. But make an ocean voyage in the Southern Hemisphere outside the tropics, and it is probable that you will see one, ten, even hundreds of these magical birds. Better still, visit one of their island nesting colonies, perhaps at the Falklands, Galápagos or Taiaroa Head in New Zealand, and you will be charmed and enthralled by their trusting nature and comical clumsiness. It takes but a few seconds to realise that these huge, long-winged birds have evolved to be masters of the

The ultimate ocean wanderer, a lone albatross passes by and is soon lost over the horizon.

air at the cost of their skills on land. Even the most experienced birds have difficulty in making the transition from fast flight to land-based nesting duties, many landing forcefully in what might best be described as a dishevelled heap.

Like the majority of people, my home is very far away from albatrosses, but by remarkable chance the first seabird research trip I made as an undergraduate coincided with a nesting attempt

The exquisite features of a grey-headed albatross.

of a very lost black-browed albatross on the most northerly island in the UK – Unst in the Shetland Islands. I remember being fascinated and intrigued by this lovely, lonely creature, half a world away from home, and would often make the half-hour walk along the cliff top from my tent to gaze at it through a telescope. Little did I know then, as an eighteen-year-old, that more than 25 years later I would have the privilege of seeing full colonies of these birds in many parts of the world, and carry out

research on them. This bird, inevitably dubbed 'Albert' by those who saw it, returned to the same nest in a gannet colony every season for many years, and gave hundreds of British and European birders their first experience of a live albatross. That said, you often had to take on trust the fact that it was indeed alive, so inanimate was this bird as it brooded its imaginary egg. In many hours of watching I never saw it fly, and only years later did I understand that this was perfectly natural – black-brows typically sit for days at a time!

As with many other groups of animals, the number of albatross species and sub-species is currently the subject of much conjecture and disagreement. The picture is clouded, rather than clarified, by adding genetic evidence to the mix, not only because its greater insight is at odds with the traditional wisdom of 13 species, but because interpretation of genetic data differs between specialists. In this book I have taken the non-committal approach of recognising 24 types or taxa of albatross (listed at the back of the book) until such time as the taxonomical dust settles and a new consensus emerges. It is safer to 'split' species than to 'lump' them when there is doubt, especially when their continued existence may be dependent on management of human activity, in this case fisheries. One species could be lost completely, and without anyone realising, if it could not be distinguished from another albatross with a larger population living in the same region. A relatively small, say 10 per cent, reduction in overall numbers could actually represent the extinction of the rarer species.

Despite uncertainty about details, there is general agreement that albatrosses can be divided into four natural groups, each of which represents a different evolutionary branch of the tree. These groups – called 'mollymawks', 'sooty albatrosses', 'great albatrosses' and 'Pacific albatrosses' – are considered separately in much of the book. The fossil record indicates that the four groups, or genera, have been separate for millions of years.

Albatrosses are the very largest members of a group of seabirds aptly known as 'tubenoses' for the tubular nostrils that sit on their upper beak – evidence of a shared evolutionary ancestry. Together this large group, known as *Procellariiformes*, comprises as many as 125 species living today; the remainder being petrels, shearwaters, prions, diving petrels and storm-petrels. A feature which distinguishes albatrosses from all others in the group is that their nostrils are separated – one either side of the upper beak – whereas in all other species the nostrils are side-by-side on top of the beak. In recognition of this and other features, taxonomists long ago awarded albatrosses their own 'family', the Diomedeidae. This name derives from *Diomedea*, the collective term given to albatrosses by Linnaeus based on the mythical transformation of the companions of the Greek warrior Diomedes into birds.

The wonderfully successful 'tubenoses' branch of seabirds has colonised every ocean in the

world, and all maritime habitats from pole to pole by way of the tropics. Most island groups, however remote, and however small, have one or more species of tubenose breeding on them, and some species breed only on a single island, such is their degree of specialisation. The diversity of the tubenoses is demonstrated by their range of body size. The smallest, the storm-petrels, are typically a mere 50 g (2 oz) in weight, and 40 cm (16 in) in wingspan. The largest, the southern royal albatross, is some 200 times heavier at around 10 kg (22 lb) and has a monstrous wingspan of more than 3 m (10 ft). But body size does not tell the whole story. Although albatrosses, shearwaters, petrels and prions all glide on long wings, the stubby little diving petrels race between the waves on fast-beating wings, looking remarkably similar to little auks in the Arctic, and the dainty storm-petrels dance across the sea surface, their fluttering wings reminiscent of butterflies. Albatrosses are considered to be the ultimate ocean

Laysan albatrosses are unlike all others, but the differences are only skin deep.

wanderers, but huge migrations are a feature of most tubenoses. Even the delicate Wilson's storm-petrel, with its white rump and the characteristic yellow webbing of its feet, moves annually from Antarctic breeding grounds to the north Atlantic. Its annual migration is equivalent in distance to flying around the globe. All this in a bird little bigger than a sparrow.

Albatrosses vary in colour, size and shape, but they have a similar basic structure and form

The longest wings in the animal world allow albatrosses to glide effortlessly.

because of their shared ancestry. Most of their physical features are also common to the majority of the other tubenoses for the same reason, although shearwaters and large petrels may have diverged from the albatross lineage more recently than storm-petrels and diving petrels, judging by their greater similarity in size and behaviour. Two birds – the northern and southern giant petrels, collectively known as geeps (from GPs) to those familiar with them – are so similar to albatrosses in flight that they are often mistaken for them. But a close view of the head clears away any doubts. At the risk of offending giant petrel admirers I have to say that, unlike albatrosses, they could never be described as beautiful to the human eye. Their massive beak is designed for tearing flesh, for geeps are the vultures of the sub-Antarctic and quickly demolish seal and penguin carcasses, and such equipment is hardly conducive to a pleasing appearance except in the eye of another geep!

The basic elements of an albatross, from bottom to top, are these. Large, fully-webbed feet for swimming and shallow diving. Strong, scaled legs to support a large body weight. A long, cylindrical body with a broad tail (except in sooty albatrosses, which have a pointed tail). Long, narrow wings that can be locked straight and provide enough lift to support the bird aloft with minimal flapping. A rounded head with a long, hooked beak, and a wide gape to allow the swallowing of large food items like fish and squid without the need to cut or tear them.

At close quarters, the upper beak is seen to be made up of several different thin 'plates', reminiscent of our own fingernails and made of much the same material. These fit tightly together, and cover an underlying bony structure which is an extension of the skull. The hook itself is an impressive tool that allows the bird to grasp slippery prey or an unfortunate researcher's hand, and the cutting edge of the upper beak closes on that of the lower with a precision that would be the envy of any scissor-maker. The combination, especially in the larger species, is akin to an industrial can-opener. You mess with an albatross at your peril, as the triangular scar on my right hand – due to a moment's carelessness when checking a wandering albatross ring – bears witness.

A majestic southern royal albatross demonstrates a shared ancestry with other 'tubenosed' seabirds.

Understanding Albatrosses

Life on the Wind

A combination of age-old observation and the latest high-tech tracking devices have recently allowed even better understanding of just how albatrosses use wind and wave to move around. Global positioning system (GPS) devices are now small enough to comfortably fit on the back of an albatross, and they can be programmed to provide the location of the bird, accurate to a wingspan or two, every second. Coupled with knowledge of wind speed and direction, and wave height and direction, all available from satellites passing unseen overhead, enough information is then available to see just how the bird responds to its immediate environment on a second-by-second basis. Some stunning work on this subject has been done by Henri Weimerskirch and colleagues, who have shown that albatrosses can fly with little more effort than they use resting on land, and that they use predictable weather patterns to maximise flight efficiency, flying in long anti-clockwise loops while heading north, and clockwise loops when heading southwards.

Just how the tubenosed seabirds manage to locate patchy prey in a vast ocean was not adequately understood until quite recently. It transpires that an extraordinary sense of smell is central to their success. They can detect concentrations of an odour far below the threshold at which we would be aware of it, and then head towards the source upwind, the smell becoming more intense all the time. This characteristic is now well known among keen birdwatchers, who will head out on a small boat from places like Tasmania and New Zealand towards the shelf edge with buckets full of the most malodorous concoction of fish oil and blood that they can devise. Poured on the sea surface in a promising area, even if devoid of seabirds at the time, this fetid mixture will soon start attracting storm-petrels, petrels, shearwaters and albatrosses from a great distance downwind. Not infrequently this fishy offering is augmented by the least boat-adapted ornithologists as the combination of swell, engine fumes and noxious smell takes effect!

The Salvin's albatross uses smell to locate its prey.

Another intriguing question is how albatrosses are able to locate and return to their nest on a tiny speck of rock in a very large ocean. One theory was that they used the earth's magnetic field to navigate by, but recent research has shown this not to be the case, so the mystery remains.

The distances travelled by albatrosses during their everyday lives seem almost literally incredible to us, for whom walking or running even a few kilometres is a significant effort. Albatrosses have for centuries been famous for their travels, but the introduction of satellite tracking in the 1990s revealed a scale of movement that astonished even experienced ornithologists. Distances of 1000 km (c 625 miles) per day are not unusual, and a grey-headed albatross circumnavigated the globe, visiting waters off South America, Africa and Australia, in just 46 days.

Most albatrosses nest on oceanic islands in a narrow band around the Southern Hemisphere, roughly centred on the Roaring Forties, the windiest place on earth. This is no coincidence, for albatross flight is powered not by flapping, but by gliding, and without air movement a gliding bird can only descend. So, in general, albatrosses will be found where there is wind, and plenty of it. Wind is energy, and albatrosses and petrels use that energy to get around. Without it, they can be marooned, and satellite-tracking studies have shown that they will often sit on the sea between weather systems, patiently awaiting the assured return of wind to allow them to continue their journey.

Their comfort in windy conditions is clear during any ship journey in their realm. The rougher the weather, and the more the ship rolls, so the greater is the flying activity of albatrosses and petrels, and the more apparent is their effortless control of what, for us, are the worst conditions at sea. For the human ocean traveller there are few consolations for the discomfort of rough weather, but the joyous sight of an albatross careering across the face of steep swell like an aerial surfer, rising to meet the next roller and then skipping over its crest, is certainly one of them. Many is the time that I have clung to the railings of a ship in storm-force winds, struggling to maintain my footing, while watching albatrosses gleefully wheeling across the sky on rigid wings,

Albatrosses thrive in stormy conditions, using the wind's energy to fly prodigious distances. In calm airs they patiently sit on the sea, knowing that it's only a matter of time before the next low pressure system heads their way.

Making the transition from the air to the land is never easy for a bird that cannot flap its wings to decelerate. This black-browed albatross is about to drop heavily, using its out-stretched legs as shock absorbers.

then curving down to run along the face of a huge swell with their wing tips almost – but never quite – touching the water surface. Sometimes the same individual, identified perhaps by an errant feather on a wing, will continue to run rings around the vessel for hours on end, before seemingly tiring of the game and spiralling away in search of more interesting fare elsewhere. This efficiency of effort has received a good deal of scientific investigation, for albatrosses have enthralled sea-farers for centuries, and their stories and descriptions inspired others to seek to explain their abilities long before man discovered the secrets of flight.

Nest maintenance continues throughout the season.

Forced to Land

Although albatrosses can do most things at sea or in the air, the one element of life that forces them back to dry land is reproduction. Like all birds, their genes are passed to the next generation in the form of an egg, and even albatrosses have not yet discovered how to incubate an egg and rear a hatchling on the surface of the water. Once an albatross returns to a breeding colony after several years of juvenile wanderings, it begins the long apprenticeship that will culminate in finding a mate, constructing a nest and making a first breeding attempt. This process in itself takes several years, but it can be seen as an investment which finds its reward in hopefully many years of successful breeding with the same partner.

Young albatrosses leave the nest fully feathered, often with comical tufts of down wafting around the head and neck. Thereafter they undertake annual replacement of their body feathers, in a process known as moult, and replace their flight feathers every one to three years. In dark

species, like the black-footed and sooty albatrosses, successive annual moults leave the birds looking almost unchanged, but in most there is a gradual replacement of dark feathers by white ones. The development of full, mature adult plumage is so protracted that the age of most albatrosses up to four years is apparent from the pattern of their white feathers, especially so in the case of the great albatrosses, which may take a decade to look like a full adult. Not only do the birds differ from year to year, but it is also said that no two wandering albatrosses look exactly alike, such is the potential for small differences between them.

Although timings and details differ between species, all albatrosses broadly follow the same nesting pattern. Firstly, like most seabirds, albatrosses nest in colonies rather than individually. In the case of mollymawks and Pacific albatrosses the colonies are large and dense, with hundreds or thousands of nests in close proximity. In great albatrosses the colonies are smaller (tens or hundreds of nests) and much more spread out. And in sooty albatrosses the colonies are usually of just a handful of nests placed together on a cliff ledge. In all species, the experienced male breeders return to the nest-site shortly before females, establish a territory on and around the nest, refurbish the nest structure, which may have been damaged since the previous breeding attempt, and patiently await the arrival of their partners. Females then return, and the pair re-establish their bond and mate before the female returns to sea to feed while an egg is developing inside her oviduct.

After a week or so she returns once more to lay the large egg – always just one – and takes the first turn at incubating it while the male takes the opportunity to fly off and feed himself until it's his turn to look after the precious egg. Both sexes transfer body heat to the egg by tucking it up against their 'brood-patch' – an area of bare skin rich in blood vessels which is normally hidden by feathers, but can be deliberately exposed by the bird when needed. All albatross eggs are essentially white, incidentally, because camouflage would be pointless in such an exposed nest, but I have noticed that the larger end of wandering albatross eggs are often rufous-speckled.

Some albatross colonies contain thousands of nests, as here on Steeple Jason in the Falklands.

The change of incubation shift is amusing to watch. The off-duty bird returns to the nest after days at sea, anxious to follow its parental urge to sit on the egg. But its mate normally shows no intention to abdicate responsibility for the growing embryo, and continues to sit tight. After a while the newcomer's patience is stretched to the limit; first it tries to nudge the incumbent off the nest, and then, if that fails, climbs on its back! At this, the sitter normally takes the hint and reluctantly stands, carefully checks that the egg has been released from the brood-patch, and then climbs off the nest, to be immediately replaced by its partner. The egg or chick is exposed for no more than a few seconds – a rapid hand-over that owes more to protection from egg-thieves like skuas and sheathbills than to any risk of cooling.

The one, white egg is carefully incubated on the dish-shaped nest.

Incubation lasts for 70-80 days, the longest such period for any bird. After several exchanges of duty, it is the male that normally hatches the chick. It may take up to five days for the chick to complete the exhausting task of breaking out of its thick shell. Parents once again take turns to brood the fast-growing chick while it develops the ability to keep warm without protection from Mum or Dad. Gradually the brooding parent sits less tightly, allowing the youngster to 'harden off' on warmer days, and eventually he or she may just sit beside the nest, vigilant for potential trouble in the form of harsh weather or a predator. Finally the period of brood-guard is complete, and the chick is left to fend for itself while both parents go off foraging, sometimes covering thousands of kilometres before returning with a store of energy-rich food for the ever-hungry chick.

Both parents incubate the egg and tend the chick. Here, one parent relieves its partner of baby-sitting duties, and checks that all is well after its long journey at sea.

Transfer of the oily, stinking, part-digested food to the chick is accomplished with remarkable speed and the minimum of mess. The youngster first indicates that it is ready to accept another parcel of sustenance by pecking at its parent's bill and making little hungry noises. If the adult

Food passing from adult to youngster.

has not already been emptied out, and is in the mood, he or she will point its bill down and open it slightly, meanwhile pumping the 'nectar' up from its reservoir, the proventriculus or fore-stomach. Seeing that the meal is about to arrive, the chick increases its begging and puts its little black beak inside and across the parent's now wide-open mouth. The oily paste is then passed across from adult to chick with amazing synchrony of movement, and usually without a drop being spilled. The performance is often repeated every few minutes, especially when the chick is young and can only consume small amounts at a time. Months later, the chick is literally larger than its parent, and can consume the parent's entire delivery, which has usually taken many days and thousands of miles to collect, in a few minutes.

After a while longer, the chick begins to develop proper body feathers, and eventually it grows so large that it overtakes both parents in body weight. By this time, food deliveries are reducing in size and frequency, and for the final few weeks on the nest the youngster steadily loses weight. This seems to act as a trigger, and stimulates the chick to start exercising its wing muscles prior to fledging. In strong winds chicks open their wings, and for the first time experience the lift that these

A black-browed albatross chick eagerly awaits its next meal.

26

unwieldy, heavy appendages give. Eventually even the longest, outer flight feathers have completed their growth, the chick has slimmed to its parent's weight, and it is time to leave the sanctuary of the colony for a period of several years at sea.

Unlike some other seabirds, albatrosses do not escort or protect their fledgling after it has departed, and the youngster finally takes to the air very unsteadily, increases confidence and soars off as an independent bird for the first time. Such inexperienced birds are of course poor at finding and catching food for themselves at first, and live off the reserves of fat that their parents provided. Slowly, though, most do learn the principles of successful foraging, perhaps by following other more experienced albatrosses, and they disperse over vast areas. For reasons of bad weather, poor food supplies, disease, predation or simple inexperience, this post-fledging period is the most dangerous of their lives, and many perish. But the strongest, fittest and luckiest do survive, and go on to join the large segment of albatross populations that are not yet old enough to breed. Without ties to land or a nesting timetable to follow, these juveniles wander freely over vast areas of ocean, and it is usually from this class of birds that we get the odd-ball 'lost' albatrosses that turn up very far away from the normal range of the species. One of the most spectacular examples of such wayward behaviour in recent years was the appearance in the northern North Atlantic of several young yellow-nosed albatrosses in 2007. Breeding on Tristan da Cunha and Gough Island south of the Equator, a number of birds crossed the tropics and were seen off the coasts of the United States, Sweden, Norway and Britain. Two were found exhausted and taken into care, but quickly recovered and were subsequently released back to the wild.

The rare appearance of lost albatrosses in the only ocean without a breeding population raises the question as to why the North Atlantic is apparently unable to sustain them. This anomaly is all the more intriguing because sub-fossil remains show that albatrosses did indeed once breed on the coasts of Bermuda and North Carolina, but became extinct there less than 400,000 years ago. The demise of these birds may have been due to climate change or, earlier, the closure of the sea gap between North and South America, but the question still remains as to why albatrosses today survive in every ocean except one.

One of the most remarkable characteristics of albatrosses is their return to the colony in which they hatched when they are old enough to breed. In the case of great albatrosses, it may be four or five years between leaving the colony as a newly-fledged youngster and returning to it as a sub-adult. During this time the bird may have flown far enough to reach the Moon, yet unerringly it will find a tiny speck of land in a huge ocean and likely crash-land there, often within a few metres of where it was hatched, and begin the process of pairing and learning how to produce and rear a chick of its own.

This urge to find and return to what is called the natal colony has several consequences, one of which is that this most well-travelled of birds invariably chooses a local boy or girl as a mate, and in turn this results in reproductive isolation between island groups. The strength of this behaviour is apparent in the physical differences we

A 'lost' white-capped albatross on South Georgia.

see between albatrosses of the same species-group that breed at different sites. More remarkable still, albatrosses from isolated colonies around the Southern Ocean often spend months of the year mixing and feeding in exactly the same stretch of ocean, yet almost without fail go back to their natal colony when the season dictates. Inevitably some, a tiny minority, get it wrong. I have already mentioned the black-browed and yellow-nosed albatrosses that somehow found themselves in the wrong hemisphere. There are many examples of other birds that proved to be navigationally-challenged, including a white-capped albatross (normally nesting on sub-Antarctic islands south of

New Zealand) that turned up in a black-brow colony on South Georgia between 2003 and 2010, more than 10,000 km (c 6250 miles) from 'home'. This bird, a male, occupied a nest and displayed to the black-brows nearby, but was unable to attract a mate.

The tendency to return to the natal colony has greatly helped scientists to learn such things as the age at which albatrosses first breed and how long they live. At Bird Island, South Georgia, colleagues of mine at the British Antarctic Survey have ringed many hundreds of young albatrosses each year for decades, and most of those that survive their juvenile years on the wing eventually return to the island. As a result, the vast majority of wandering albatrosses breeding here, and many black-brows and grey-heads, are of known age, their uniquely numbered rings revealing when and where they were reared. In one visit to a grey-head colony in 2007, I found three parents carrying rings that had been placed on their legs at least 30 years earlier, perhaps while they were sitting on the very same nest at which I encountered them. My first thought at the time was that these birds, each of which may have travelled a million kilometres since they had first been marked, looked just as perfect as their neighbours, some of whom would have been decades younger. The extreme longevity of albatrosses is further proven by the fact that some of the wandering albatrosses ringed at the nest on Bird Island by Lance Tickell in the 1960s are still with us today. They have outlived the original rings, and in some cases several subsequent ones have also needed replacement, but the birds themselves look as fresh and strong as they did decades ago. This is a study animal that can live longer than the professional career of their researchers.

Life in the Slow Lane

An endearing characteristic of all albatrosses, and other such long-lived birds like swans, is that they normally pair for life – 'til death do they part. Those partnerships are formed after long courtships, and reinforced by ritual greetings each time the two birds are reunited after days, weeks, or even

Courting southern royal albatrosses on Otago Peninsula, New Zealand. Pair bonds may last a lifetime.

many months of separation. During the often-long period between successfully fledging one chick and returning to the nest to lay the next egg, the two parents may be literally half a world apart but, all being well, their urge to reproduce will bring them back to the exact same spot on a remote island within a few days of each other.

Among the planet's animals and plants there are species which live life in the fast lane – grow quickly, reproduce early and die young – and those that do so at a far more leisurely pace. Among birds, albatrosses are very firmly in the slow lane. They may take a decade or more to reproduce for the first time, may produce but one egg every two years and, barring accident or disease, will still be nesting in their 40s. Contrast this strategy, for example, with most garden birds with which we are familiar. They nest at age one, may produce two clutches of ten eggs per year, and nearly all will be dead before an albatross is thinking seriously about making its first nest. Ironically, a female of either species will on average leave the same number of surviving offspring to carry their genes into the future, but the manner in which they achieve this clearly differs enormously. These extreme examples of how populations work, and everything in-between, can be considered as strategies. Such strategies are the consequence of millions of years of evolution, driven by the greater reproductive success of the individuals that behave or are shaped slightly differently, and slightly in better harmony with their environment, than their neighbours.

Many bird species nest several times a year, most do so once a year, and a small minority nest less than once per year. It is, however, quite common for albatrosses to nest but once every two years (called biennial breeding), and this is normal for the great albatrosses, the two species of sooties, and for one mollymawk – the grey-headed albatross. If the egg is lost, or the chick dies in the nest, then biennial breeders will often try again a year later. But if the chick fledges successfully, the parents go to sea for a year, probably not touching land in all that time, and enjoy a well-earned rest after many months of delivering food to their demanding chick.

This light-mantled sooty albatross must patiently incubate its egg for many weeks.

The World's Albatrosses

Pacific Albatrosses

This group of four albatrosses includes the only one to nest in the tropics (Galápagos albatross), and the only ones to nest in the northern hemisphere (Laysan, black-footed and short-tailed albatrosses). Despite their outward dissimilarities, the Pacific albatrosses are genetically more similar to each than to any of the southern albatrosses, and are thought to share a common ancestor – very likely a bird that originated in the Southern Ocean. That separation has been shown by the fossil record to have occurred in the middle Miocene (12-15 million years ago). Equally remarkable is that remains of albatrosses of this group have been found at what were once colonies in the North Atlantic, a region in which there are sadly no breeding albatrosses today.

The Galápagos albatross is a comical-looking bird with prominent brows and a very long, yellow beak. It breeds on only two islands, Isla Española in the Galápagos archipelago and Isla de la Plata off the coast of Ecuador, and has the smallest oceanic range of any albatross. Given that albatrosses require wind to move around, and that the tropics are notorious for gentle airs, it is surprising to many that the species is able to survive at such low latitudes at all. Outside the breeding season, birds move away from the Galápagos to the south and east, and make a living towards the coast of South America. This species is remarkable in that in most cases it makes no nest at all, and may shuffle its egg around the colony, sometimes moving it tens of metres from where it was laid.

The Hawaiian-nesting Laysan and black-footed albatrosses are known locally as Goonies, the name originally being a term of fun, but now one of endearment. The Laysan albatross was a victim of over-harvesting for feathers in the early twentieth century. It survived such deprivations partly due to its wide breeding range, which covers much of the Pacific Ocean along the Tropic of Cancer.

The short-tailed albatross, also known as Steller's albatross, is the rarest albatross alive today, and owes its very existence to the fact that it takes many years to mature and breed. This species

The Galápagos, or waved, albatross makes no nest, and must endure high temperatures.

was hunted on an industrial scale for its feathers, literally tonnes of which were transported by light railway from one of its main colonies, to the extent that all breeding birds had been killed by the 1940s. No eggs at all were laid for some years, but this was a blessing in disguise because the tradition of collecting feathers died with the colony. When, in 1954, an egg was laid by birds that in all likelihood had escaped the killing by virtue of being at sea in their juvenile years, the local human culture had changed, and thereafter the species received protection. Today, the total population exceeds 2,000 birds, and the species is slowly climbing away from what seemed likely extinction only half a century ago. It now breeds on two Japanese islands, and should continue its recovery if it remains free of significant fishery by-catch, as it does now. Much of the credit for this success story is due to Hiroshi Hasegawa, a Japanese ornithologist whose life's work has been the protection and nurturing of short-tailed albatross colonies on these two tiny, remote islands.

Today, the majority of nests of this species occur on the steep slopes of the small volcanic island of Torishima. They are often destroyed by land-slips after monsoon rainfall, and are vulnerable to further eruptions of the still-active volcano. The risk of another catastrophic decline in this albatross would be greatly reduced if some could be persuaded to breed elsewhere, and in early 2008 the first steps were taken to bring this about. Ten large chicks were flown to a safe island where the species once bred, the aim being that they will fly from here as juveniles and return to their new home to start a new colony in a few years time.

The fascinating recent discovery of fossilised bones and eggshells of this species in Bermuda, dated about 400,000 years old, shows that the short-tailed albatross used to breed in the North Atlantic and therefore had a hugely wider distribution than today.

Mollymawks

A group of eleven similar-sized and similar-shaped albatrosses, with wing-spans of around 2 m (6½ ft), share the genus *Thalassarche* and are collectively known as mollymawks or mollies. This rather uncomplimentary name hardly does justice to some of the most beautiful of all

The short-tailed, or Stellar's, albatross is climbing back from the brink of extinction after being harvested for its feathers. Confined to the Pacific Ocean today, archaeologists have shown that this species once nested in the North Atlantic.

seabirds. The delicate face patterns and strikingly coloured beaks are breathtaking at close quarters. The group spans the Southern Ocean, and one or more species nests on almost every sub-Antarctic archipelago, the birds fanning out to cover much of the Southern Hemisphere outside the breeding season.

Mollies usually nest in dense colonies, up to 100,000 strong, and often on slopes and crags to allow birds to arrive and depart using the wind for a steep descent and near-vertical take-off. Nests are frequently so close together that a runway take-off, favoured by the much heavier wandering albatrosses, is simply not available. Clambering between the nests of irritable neighbours to gain a better launching spot inevitably involves harassment and pecks that are best avoided, so there is strong competition for the better nest-sites. Arrival in these dense colonies, hazardous enough because albatrosses cannot flap their wings to slow down, is made more traumatic because neighbours will peck any bird that strays into reach of their nest. To announce their imminent arrival, mollies cry out with a piercing wail in the second or two before they hit the cliff ('landing' would be a generous description of most arrivals), so at least the mate and immediate neighbours have some warning of an imminent controlled crash.

Nests are beautifully crafted tall mounds of peat or soil, with almost vertical sides and a perfect saucer-shaped depression on the top. These works of art are extremely durable, lasting for many years, and enhanced each season when the pair returns from sea to lay their single egg. The oldest nests attract lichens, and may have been first constructed decades earlier. Mollies seem to prefer wet areas, even when well-drained ground is available, and this certainly helps in nest-building, when wet soil or peat is easily crafted to build or repair the nest. So similar are the nests and behaviour of the different albatrosses in this group that they sometimes nest together, though usually in patches of their own kind.

Once the parents have abandoned brood-guard, mollie chicks of just a few weeks old must fend off the attentions of potential predators such as skuas. They do this with a remarkably effective combination of bravado and stomach oil, the latter being held back from the last meal they

received. This foul-smelling oil can have fatal consequences to a winged predator, because it clogs feathers and can break down the essential insulation that keeps the birds alive in a cold environment. For this reason, otherwise defenceless chicks of most albatross species are infrequently taken, despite them representing a fantastic source of energy-rich food. There are exceptions, however. Skuas will take advantage of any hatchling that has been left unattended by parents at too young an age, and regularly kill a large proportion of light-mantled sooty albatross chicks, probably because they lack the protection afforded by a large colony.

Like fluffy white sentries, young grey-headed albatrosses defiantly face intruders

The sight of a black-browed or grey-headed albatross colony in early February always brings a smile to my face. The youngsters are by now alone, and they bravely confront the intrusion by making themselves look as tall as possible, each on their identical pedestal of a nest. At this stage the chicks are pear-shaped, essentially a fluffy stomach with a beak attached, ready to receive the copious quantities of semi-digested krill, fish or squid brought back by their parents at intervals of a few days. If a potential predator approaches too closely, the youngster will repeatedly snap its beak loudly as a warning. You, as a perceived threat, receive this synchronised welcome from every chick in the colony, every one of them swivelling to keep facing you as you move gently between them, the noise of a hundred clapping beaks sounding just like the staccato plucked strings of an orchestra. Then, when truly frightened, a chick will let go with a jet of orange liquid, often liberally sprinkled with bits of semi-digested food,

A shy albatross leaves its colony. Like all mollymawks, this species nests in close proximity to others, despite constant squabbles with its nearest neighbours.

with a musty odour that lingers on the clothes, and the memory, for years. This habit of spitting oil is, incidentally, common to most petrels and storm-petrels. It is a hugely successful means of deterring predators. I am still mentally scarred from the occasions as a young ornithologist when, climbing cliffs to put rings on young fulmars without sufficient caution, I received a face-full of deterrent on suddenly coming nose-to-nose with a belligerent fulmar chick.

On the other side of the world from South Georgia, but at a very similar latitude, lies Campbell Island – famous for two species of bird that breed nowhere else, and they could hardly be more different from each other. One, a duck (the Campbell Island teal), is completely flightless and has just been saved from extinction by the removal of introduced rats on the Island by the New Zealand Government's Department of Conservation. The other, the Campbell albatross, is one of the

The yellow eye of the Campbell albatross.

world's most competent fliers. This variety of albatross is superficially extremely similar to the black-brows of South Georgia, but a close view of the head reveals a much more accentuated brow, giving a severe appearance, and the bright yellow eye is almost sinister.

The grey-headed albatross has breeding colonies scattered throughout the Southern Ocean. Uniquely among the mollymawks, it is a biennial breeder, taking a year off after successfully fledging a chick. During this sabbatical the adults can travel extraordinary distances, visiting well-known

The grey-headed albatross breeds on many islands around the Southern Ocean.

feeding areas in many parts of the Southern Ocean. One bird fitted with a small tracking device at South Georgia by colleagues at the British Antarctic Survey completed a double-circumnavigation of the Antarctic continent before returning to the breeding colony 18 months after it set out.

Five mollymawks – grey-headed, Pacific, Buller's and the two yellow-nosed albatrosses (Indian and Atlantic) – look very similar. All have black beaks with a striking yellow and orange stripe running the length of it, top and bottom. Another four are genetically closely related, have heavier beaks than the rest, and breed around the South Island of New Zealand and off Tasmania. These are the white-capped and shy albatrosses, Salvin's albatross which closely resembles these two, and the Chatham albatross. The latter, named for the archipelago where it nests, is the same shape and size as the others, but has a grey head and neck with dark brows.

Atlantic yellow-nosed albatrosses on Amsterdam Island.

The black-browed albatross vies with the Laysan for being the most numerous albatross of all. Current estimates indicate that there are some 700,000 breeding pairs, which probably represents about two million birds in total. But, as we will see later in the book, this number is being reduced at an alarming rate by deaths caused by fisheries, so what may seem to be a healthy number of birds masks a worrying downward trend.

Sooty Albatrosses

All albatrosses are magnificent, elegant fliers, but the two species of sooty albatrosses are exceptional even in this exalted company. They are immediately recognisable by their pointed tails

One of the most striking of the mollymawks, the Chatham albatross is named after the archipelago where it nests off the southeast coast of New Zealand.

The characteristic tail shape and body colour sets the light-mantled sooty albatross apart from all others. Its eerie cry echoes around the bays of South Georgia in summer.

and unusually narrow wings, and around the breeding islands are the only albatrosses that call loudly in flight and on the nesting ledge. This haunting, mournful 'reee-aaaaaaagh' cry, and the exquisite *pas de deux* which pairs describe while wheeling around the cliffs, are life-long memories for anyone lucky enough to visit nesting islands.

The two species in this group – the sooty and the light-mantled sooty do share a few breeding sites, but for the most part the former prefers more northerly waters than the latter. Sooty albatrosses are a chocolate-brown all over, while their light-mantled cousins are a smoky grey on the back, sides and belly. Their pattern of coloration, and the subtle merging of greys and browns, is reminiscent of a Siamese cat. At close quarters, these albatrosses can be seen to have a narrow line running the length of the beak – yellow in the sooty, and light blue in the light-mantled species.

Sooty albatrosses are unusual in that they breed in small groups of one to five closely-spaced nests, often a distance from the next cluster. Nests are very similar to those of mollymawks – perfect columns of peat with a bird-sized dish at the top – and they too last for many years. Nest sites are invariably on narrow ledges above cliffs, allowing birds to arrive and leave with the minimum of fuss, and without the need to tangle with neighbours. The piercing call of light-mantled sooties is heard throughout the breeding season, mainly because immature birds use it to loudly advertise their presence on potential nesting ledges to any of their species passing by. An hour spent watching these mesmerising birds languidly cruising around the cliffs of South Georgia will show much coming and going, as each bird seems to take its turn in landing and crooning to potential mates cruising past. The shrill cry is uttered with the head thrown dramatically back, and beak pointed to the sky. It is preceded by head-bobbing and head-shaking, as the newly-landed bird establishes itself on its ledge and waits for an audience. Sooty chicks are charming bundles of fluff with a white face mask and black eyes. Charming, that is, until you venture too close, when the endearing little creature will quickly demonstrate what he or she has been fed by its parents over the past few days! Despite their malodorous defence strategy, unattended light-mantled sooty chicks

are very vulnerable to predation to skuas. This may well be because, unlike other small albatrosses, they do not benefit from the mutual defence of a whole colony of birds around them. In bad years, fewer than 10 per cent of eggs laid result in chicks fledged, and since they are biennial breeders, half the adults don't even attempt to breed in any given year. The fact that the species remains still quite healthy is, therefore, testament to how long-lived are the adults. On average, more than 97 out of every 100 birds alive at the beginning of a year will live to see it out. This happy state of affairs is partly due to the fact that light-mantled sooty albatrosses mostly feed away from the areas where they might be vulnerable to entanglement in fishing gear. Satellite-tracking studies have shown that they forage further towards the ice-edge than all other species, and therefore have a long commute between breeding and feeding areas. A single round-trip is often the equivalent of flying from New York to Rome. Sooties nest at Tristan da Cunha and Gough Islands in the South Atlantic, and at four sites in the Southern Indian Ocean. Light-mantled sooties share the Indian Ocean sites, and also breed at South Georgia, Macquarie and the New Zealand sub-Antarctic islands.

Great Albatrosses

Superficially similar to each other, the largest albatrosses have now been recognised as a group of many distinct forms, perhaps representing seven different species in two sub-groups – wandering albatrosses and royal albatrosses. Many are very difficult to tell apart at sea, partly because of considerable variation within each species. Furthermore, although most nest separately, they all share vast tracts of the Southern Ocean, so no birdwatcher can be confident of which type of albatross they've seen without close examination of such tiny details as the angle of the nostrils and whether there is a line of colour on the edge of the beak. Identifying great albatrosses on the wing is not for the faint-hearted, especially when the sighting platform is normally lurching up and down, side-to-side in a typical Southern Ocean swell!

All albatrosses are large birds, but the great albatrosses are truly enormous – very much the jumbo-jets of the seabird world. Their stiff wings, curved downwards, flex in much the same

*Southern royal albatrosses displaying on Campbell Island. Flamboyant posturing
and noisy chattering between the participants are characteristic of such groups across
all great albatross species, and a vital part of courtship.*

way as do those of a large passenger plane in turbulence, and their white cylindrical bodies are also reminiscent of an aircraft. At sea, wandering and royal albatrosses seem disdainful, continuing their methodical searching pattern without any obvious attention to any other birds in their vicinity. Sometimes one or two will circle a ship for hours at a time, looking through the bridge windows as they pass by, while at other times they appear out of the mist and pass on quickly, never to be seen again.

A charming characteristic that sets great albatrosses apart from all others is an elaborate courtship display which includes a host of ritual, noisy behaviours and often involves five or more birds, many of them youngsters. The outstretched-wing display is perhaps the best-known of these behaviours, partly because this is the time when human observers appreciate the enormous wingspan of these birds. On one occasion, when I was stretched out on the ground to photograph a displaying pair, the male circled in my direction and stopped in front at arm's length, with *his* arm curving gracefully out over my head like a ballet dancer's and ending at my waist. These are wings of truly *gigantic* proportions; the longest of any bird in the world. The grandiose gestures are accompanied by a huge variety of sounds, including bill-rattling, bill-snapping, crooning and wailing. The open-wing posture is normally accompanied by a series of explosive, exultant cries with the head thrown up to the vertical, the bird circling his intended fancy like a bullfighter targeting his adversary. Bill-rattling involves a rapid series of hollow claps produced by opening and closing the huge beak in the manner of castanets, bubbling to a crescendo, and can be produced simultaneously by two or more birds, the sound travelling far across the colony and often enticing others to join the excitement.

Great albatrosses need relatively flat ground to display on, and these communal areas are usually in the midst of a nesting colony. White dots scattered around adjacent hillsides and valleys, resembling the last pockets of winter snow, are actually incubating adults that have weightier things on their mind than socialising with neighbours. Around the edges of the display arenas are half-constructed nests, on which sit or stand hopeful young males waiting for unattached females to come by, each greeted by the same cacophony, dramatic gestures and clumsy dances.

The question of how many species / sub-species / races of great albatrosses exist is particularly contentious. Originally considered to comprise just two – wandering and royal – the recent tendency is to recognise the birds of each island group as separate from each other. We therefore now have Antipodes, Amsterdam and Tristan albatrosses, nesting on their respective archipelagos, and Gibson's albatross which nests in the Auckland Islands south of New Zealand, all of which were formally classified as wandering albatrosses. No matter what nomenclature is decided, recognition that the breeding populations of each of these archipelagos are separate from each other is an important step for conservation. Alarm bells now start ringing when any such population is diminishing in size, whereas until recently this may not have occurred if the birds were wrongly considered to be but part of a widely-spread breeding species.

Up close, the apparently white plumage of a wandering albatross can be seen to include delicate vermiculation – faint wavy grey or black stripes across a feather. The degree of this patterning varies between individuals, but is generally more prevalent in younger than older birds, and in females rather than males, so the older males are usually the most pure white of all.

A strange characteristic of wandering albatrosses is a pink, damp-looking patch which occurs 'behind the ears' of some adults, especially at sea or when they have recently returned to land. The cause of this patch has been the subject of much conjecture, since it is so variable and is not part of the feather's natural pigmentation. The most likely explanation is that salt water droplets naturally exuded from the nostrils (this is how seabirds lose excess salt derived from their salty food) are pigmented by squid in the diet, flow backwards as the bird flies and evaporate on this patch of feathers, leaving just a very salty pink patch behind. To test this theory, I put some of this pink residue to the tip of my tongue, and can confirm that it is *very* salty. I can also attest that I might lose my ear if I have to repeat the experiment!

Wandering albatrosses often have a pink patch of feathers behind the ear.

Studying Albatrosses

Until half a century ago, albatrosses were known mostly from legend, poetry and mariners' tales, together with descriptions and illustrations by dedicated amateur naturalists such as Edward Wilson, who twice sailed with Capt Robert Scott to the Antarctic early in the twentieth century. The remote breeding sites of albatrosses, and the vast open oceans over which they disappeared for most of the year, were formidable barriers to learning much about them. Most people who came across albatrosses – fishermen, sealers, whalers and inhabitants of some remote islands – saw them, and their eggs, largely as a source of food. But titbits of anecdotal information gave tantalising glimpses of the extraordinary lives of these birds. One such was the capture of a wandering albatross off the coast of Chile on December 30th 1847, the bird being found to have a vial tied around its neck. Inside the vial was a note written by a frustrated whaler just 22 days earlier, saying that his ship had not caught a whale in four months, and giving his location at 5,460 km (2,950 nautical miles) to the west. The bird had therefore travelled a minimum of 250 km (134 nautical miles) per day during the intervening time. No wonder seafarers were in such awe of these huge white birds.

The wandering albatross is one of the most studied.

The first substantial scientific programme at a nesting colony was initiated by Lance Tickell at Bird Island, off South Georgia in the South Atlantic in 1958. Tickell and his colleagues put uniquely-numbered rings on the legs of thousands of albatrosses to learn about their movements and migrations, studied courtship, breeding behaviour, diet and chick growth, and a host of

The black-footed is one of only three albatross species which range into the northern hemisphere. Breeding on the low and flat north-western islands of the Hawaiian archipelago, satellite-linked transmitters carried by black-footed albatrosses show that they cover much of the vast North Pacific Ocean in their search for food.

other elements of the biology of the four species that breed on the island. His work was later followed up by scientists of the British Antarctic Survey, especially Peter Prince, John Croxall and Richard Phillips, and continues to this day as the longest-running study of albatrosses in the world. One of the major discoveries of this work – that albatrosses have extremely long lives – is beautifully illustrated by the fact that some of the birds ringed by Tickell are still alive to this day.

A huge amount of information can be gained by studying these birds at their nests, and land-based studies can show much about what they do at sea, partly through the recovery details of ringed birds found on beaches by the public, or captured at sea by fishermen. But a great leap forward in understanding was made when electronic tracking devices could be made small enough to fit on the back of an albatross, giving details of the bird's movements rather than just the start and end points, as with ringing.

Three different types of device have given the most revealing insights – satellite-linked radio transmitters, GPS loggers and geolocators. The latter are small (2 to 5 g, or less than ¼ oz), relatively cheap, and are routinely fitted to leg rings. They record the ambient light level every 10 minutes or so, and must be retrieved from the bird so these data can be downloaded. The absolute time of dawn and dusk reveals the longitude of the bird on any particular day and, apart from near the spring and autumn equinoxes, the length of daylight tells us the latitude. These clever devices can work for up to seven years – long enough to follow a fledgling albatross from the day it leaves the nest until the day it returns to land before breeding.

GPS loggers are based on the same technology as the instruments used in cars to help drivers find their way around, or by walkers to know where they are, except that the albatross carrying the device is not trained to read it! GPS loggers use satellite signals to calculate very precisely where they are on the earth's surface, and then they either simply store this information for later retrieval by the researcher when the bird returns to the nest, or they transmit it back up to another satellite. Either way, these tiny devices provide a highly detailed track of the albatross for days or

Buller's albatross – here courting on Snares Island, New Zealand – are closely related to Pacific mollymawks.

weeks. The other instrument commonly used to track seabirds – satellite transmitters – send signals back to a lab from the bird, so information on the whereabouts of the albatross is received immediately and without any need to recapture it. The transmitter is no larger than a box of matches, and it nestles down in the feathers on the back between the wings with just a thin antenna showing, yet this device is able to send radio signals to passing satellites 800 km (500 miles) overhead. How things have moved on since that whaler tied his message around the neck of his albatross more than a century and a half ago.

Another research field that has yielded revolutionary new insights into albatross biology in recent decades is that of genetics. The information locked up in their DNA has allowed us to better understand such diverse topics as their evolution over millions of years, the number of species or 'types' of albatross alive today, and the relationship between individuals in a colony. All this can be gained from a single drop of blood or a dropped feather, and the diagnostic techniques applied are much the same as those that have transformed human forensic science over the same period.

Save the Albatross

Public recognition of the desperate plight of whales launched the environmental movement in the 1970s, and was an important element in bringing about international action that resulted in the ongoing recovery of many whale populations. Two decades later, another iconic creature of the open ocean – the albatross – was found to be in deep trouble as a consequence of man's thoughtless rush to exploit a marine harvest. In this case the damage was / is not deliberate, in that albatrosses are not the target, but they and other seabirds are nonetheless being killed in vast numbers every year, at the rate of one drowning every five minutes somewhere in the world. The cause of the problem is the accidental capture of seabirds during fishing operations, and in particular during the use of gear called longlines.

As the name suggests, longlines are indeed long, and their lines are festooned with large hooks, which are baited before being sent over the stern of ocean-going ships. The hooks might then sink to the bottom, or be suspended in mid-water, for several hours of 'soak-time' before the line, hooks, hooked fish and any hooked birds, are hauled back on board the ship. The number of such baited hooks deployed each year is almost beyond imagination – in the tens of millions – and every one has the potential to kill a seabird. A typical fishing vessel might set 15,000 hooks per day, with 1.5 m (5 ft) between hooks, giving a total line length in excess of 22 km (12 miles).

The routine monitoring of albatross colonies across the world had been established for many years when, in the early 1990s, researchers at several sites began to notice some worrying changes in their study colonies. Fluctuations from year to year are commonplace in wild animal populations, and the number of occupied nests sometimes varied due to unusually bad weather or perhaps a surfeit of food near a colony, but several teams noticed what seemed to be a sustained downward trend in the number of nesting pairs. In long-lived animals like albatrosses, even several years of complete breeding failure can be overcome because the vast majority of adults will return to try again in subsequent seasons, but in this case something more sinister seemed to be involved, because many of those very birds were not even returning to the colony to lay eggs. Nests that had been in regular use for decades were lying empty, or birds would return to the nest and wait in vain for their partners of many years to appear.

Like all seabirds, albatrosses and their close relatives the petrels are quick to seize any opportunity for feeding. Their daily lives are spent covering huge expanses of almost-empty sea looking for the slightest signs of available prey, and fishing boats must be an unmistakable target – the equivalent of a flashing neon light above a fast-food restaurant. Fishing boats have always held the potential for an easy meal, as fish are often spilled when nets are hauled on board, and sometimes huge quantities of offal are poured into the sea from processing plants on board. Such easy pickings sometimes resulted in casualties, as birds were caught in winch-wires or the nets themselves, but large-scale mortality was relatively unusual. This all changed with the introduction of industrial-scale longlining. Birds are attracted to the setting of the gear, which lasts for hours, rather than the retrieval of the catch which rarely took more than a few minutes with trawling.

Once it had been recognised, the near-universal downward spiral in albatross numbers provoked huge concern around the world, and demands for measures to reduce and halt the needless deaths of these iconic birds. With remarkable speed, a co-ordinated programme of research, publicity events and education of both the public and fishery organisations was mounted by Birdlife International, a partnership of bird conservation organisations around the world, and the Save the Albatross Campaign was born. Reacting to public opinion and the irrefutable evidence of what was causing the problem, governments of many nations negotiated a new treaty to tackle it. The Agreement on the Conservation of Albatrosses and Petrels (ACAP) has a scientific advisory council to keep abreast of the rapidly changing situation in the many fisheries and seabird populations around the world, and meets annually to agree on what action should be taken. Simultaneously, fishing boat owners and fishery regulators worked to find ways of reducing seabird mortality while minimising any negative impact on the number of fish caught. Trials were made using different types of lines, methods of scaring birds away from the danger area behind the ship, ways of hiding the baited hooks from the birds before they sank, and even dyes to make the bait look less attractive to birds (blue seemed to work best).

The good news is that effective measures can easily be taken to reduce albatross and petrel bycatch to insignificant levels. An example of what can be achieved with co-operation between government and the fishing industry is evident in what has occurred around South Georgia in the past decade, home to more than a hundred thousand pairs of albatrosses of four species. Before mitigation measures were introduced, many thousands of albatrosses and petrels were dying annually in longline and trawl fisheries around the island. Today, the fisheries continue, but the killing of seabirds has been eliminated. This has been achieved through a number of regulations that must be obeyed by any fishing boat obtaining a licence to fish in South Georgia waters. They include only setting longlines at night, putting extra weights on the lines so the hooks sink quickly, and trailing coloured streamers to frighten birds away from the bait while it is near the surface. Trawlers, too,

The endangered sooty albatross.

can kill albatrosses that become entangled in their warp lines (the steel cables that pull the net along), especially if offal from the previous catch is being discharged over the side while the net is being towed, thereby attracting birds from far and wide to concentrate in the danger area. But, again, simple measures will dramatically reduce the number of seabird deaths, in this case by preventing offal discharge during towing of the net, and trailing streamers above the warp lines.

The bad news is that, despite the availability of readily available equipment to reduce bycatch, the fishing fleets of many nations continue to operate without it. Perhaps through ignorance in

some cases, and certainly through a lack of concern in others. Ships flying the flags of Uruguay, Argentina, France, Japan and other developed nations continue to kill albatrosses and petrels at frightening rates.

The urgency of the situation is in no doubt. I'm writing these words on a ship on the way home from South Georgia, where we have just discovered that the number of breeding wandering albatrosses has declined 13 per cent since the last time these birds nested two years ago. The colony is little more than a quarter of what it was 30 years ago, and at the current rate this most glorious bird will be perilously close to extinction in less than two decades.

But a solution is at hand, and we can all help to stop this madness of unnecessary killing. First, support the 'Save the Albatross' campaign through your Birdlife International partner organisation (the RSPB in the UK, Audubon in the U.S., Bird Studies Canada in Canada, Birds Australia in Australia and Forest & Bird in New Zealand). Second, whenever possible buy fish from fisheries that have earned the Marine Stewardship Council label – these are sustainable, well-managed fisheries that do not kill significant numbers of albatrosses or dolphins.

The problem faced by albatrosses and petrels is real and desperately urgent. But thankfully it has been recognised early enough, and solutions have been found, such that the killing can be stopped before it is too late, and it must be. Most albatrosses around the world today have a very real chance of dying a ghastly death on a hook until this menace is beaten.

Changing Attitudes and Hope for the Future

The manuscript for this book was completed during a two-month stay on South Georgia. I was leading a project to restore the island's ecology by eradicating predatory rats, thereby allowing millions of seabirds to reclaim their ancestral home. The rats had been accidentally introduced by humans over two centuries of exploitation of South Georgia's magnificent marine wildlife – seals, whales and fish – with devastating consequences.

During this trip the longline fishing season started, and two licensed boats came in to

King Edward Cove to be inspected. Each carried an official observer to enforce regulations and report any accidental albatross deaths, though these are very rare in South Georgia waters now. On the shores of that same cove are the derelict remains of Grytviken whaling station. Within my lifetime those waters had been coloured crimson with the blood of whales being processed, the populations being saved from extinction only because the industry died first.

The sight of a gleaming vessel representing today's highly-regulated marine harvest at South Georgia against the backdrop of a rusting monument to yesteryear's mismanaged equivalent was striking. The very fact that I was on the island as part of a team undoing damage wrought by previous generations of visitors to South Georgia was further demonstration of how public perception has changed. Unsustainable harvesting of marine resources for food or industry is no longer acceptable in most parts of the developed world. Neither is the accidental killing of albatrosses, dolphins, turtles or sharks in pursuit of the main prey, whether it's toothfish off South Georgia, tuna off South Africa or any other marine harvest around the world. And there are thousands of people who feel so strongly about man's past shameful damage to South Georgia's wildlife that they are prepared to help turn the clock back. The island's Habitat Restoration Project, run by the South Georgia Heritage Trust, is one of the world's largest privately-funded wildlife conservation operations. It is supported by people of many nationalities, including many who are fortunate enough to visit the island and are inspired by its harsh beauty and the chance to give South Georgia's wildlife a brighter future.

Of course, it is not all good news. Albatrosses are still being killed by the thousands in other fisheries, and even South Georgia populations continue to decline because of this, but the tide is turning. Just as commercial whaling and the killing of dolphins in the pursuit of tuna have been dramatically curtailed as a result of public pressure, soon I trust will also be the killing of albatrosses and petrels in fisheries around the southern hemisphere. We do have time – a very short time – to save the albatross, a challenge we can and must meet. Future generations will neither understand nor forgive if we carelessly lose this iconic ocean wanderer, whose fate is entirely in our hands.

ARCTIC CIRCLE

Oceanic Wanderers

The development of small electronic devices that can track the movements of albatrosses at sea has revolutionised our understanding of their extraordinary way of life. This map shows the positions of hundreds of birds over periods of weeks or months, with albatrosses of each species represented by a different colour. See how the tracks are clustered in the middle latitudes of both northern and southern hemispheres (the 'Roaring Forties' and 'Furious Fifties' where winds are strongest), whereas very few albatrosses spend time in the calm airs of the tropics. The Northern Indian Ocean and North Atlantic have no albatross populations today, although they did breed in the North Atlantic thousands of years ago. Overwhelmingly, albatrosses are creatures of the Southern Ocean, where the westerly winds are unimpeded by land.

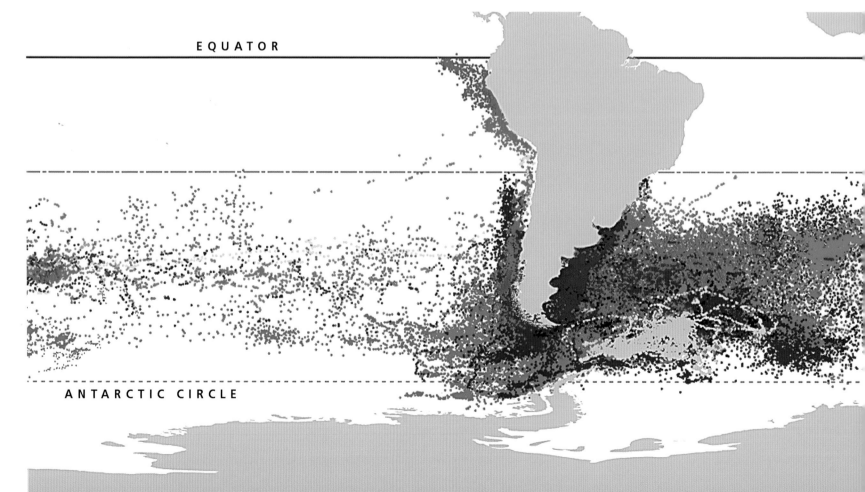

EQUATOR

ANTARCTIC CIRCLE

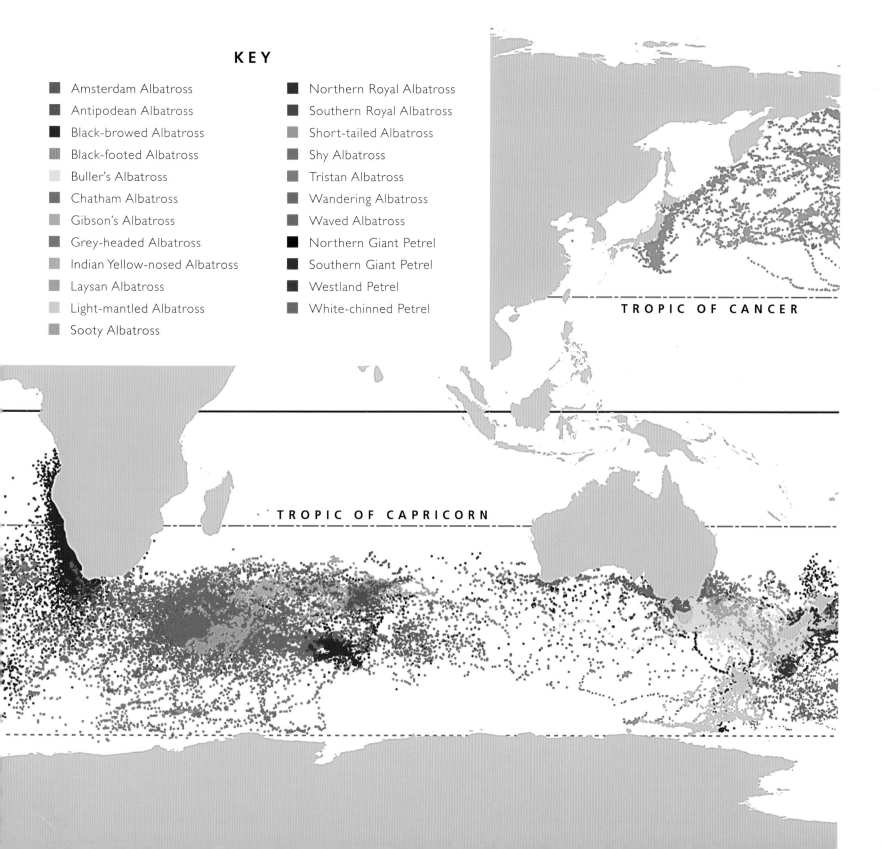

KEY

- Amsterdam Albatross
- Antipodean Albatross
- Black-browed Albatross
- Black-footed Albatross
- Buller's Albatross
- Chatham Albatross
- Gibson's Albatross
- Grey-headed Albatross
- Indian Yellow-nosed Albatross
- Laysan Albatross
- Light-mantled Albatross
- Sooty Albatross
- Northern Royal Albatross
- Southern Royal Albatross
- Short-tailed Albatross
- Shy Albatross
- Tristan Albatross
- Wandering Albatross
- Waved Albatross
- Northern Giant Petrel
- Southern Giant Petrel
- Westland Petrel
- White-chinned Petrel

TROPIC OF CANCER

TROPIC OF CAPRICORN

Oceanic Wanderers – Grey-headed Albatrosses

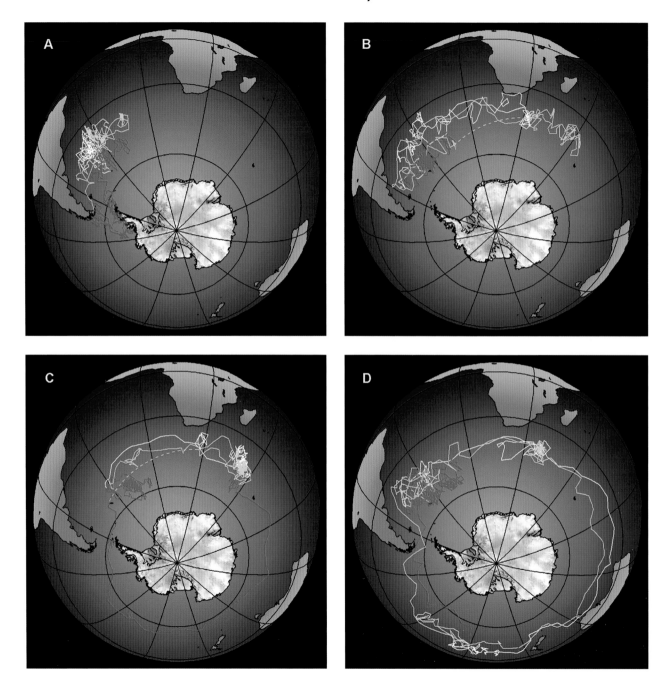

Covering unimaginable distances, these are the tracks of four grey-headed albatrosses followed by satellite in the 18 months between breeding seasons. White and yellow lines show movements in winter; red lines represent summer. Bird D circumnavigated the entire Antarctic continent twice! One albatross flew around the world in just 46 days.

Albatross Facts

	Scientific Name	Nesting Sites	Population Size (pairs)	Trend/Status	Max Wing-span
GREAT ALBATROSSES					
Wandering albatross	*Diomedea exulans*	Southern Ocean islands, esp Crozet, Prince Edward & S Georgia	26,000	declining	3.7m
Antipodean albatross	*Diomedea antipodensis*	Islands S of New Zealand, esp Antipodes and Auckland Islands	12,500	declining	3.5m
Amsterdam albatross	*Diomedea amsterdamensis*	Amsterdam Island, S Indian Ocean	25	critically endangered	3.4m
Tristan albatross	*Diomedea dabbenena*	Gough Island, S Atlantic Ocean	1,500	critically endangered	3.5m
Northern royal albatross	*Diomedea sanfordi*	Around southern New Zealand, esp Chatham Islands	7,000	declining	3.1m
Southern royal albatross	*Diomedea epomophora*	Most on Campbell Island, south of New Zealand	8,500	not known	3.0m
Gibson's albatross	*Diomedea gibsoni*	Auckland Islands, New Zealand	10,000	not known	3.5m
NORTH PACIFIC ALBATROSSES					
Galápagos (waved) albatross	*Phoebastria irrorata*	Mostly on Española Island, Galápagos archipelago	35,000	slight decline	2.3m
Short-tailed (Steller's) albatross	*Phoebastria albatrus*	Torishima Island and Senkaku Retto, western N Pacific Ocean	470	increasing	2.3m
Black-footed albatross	*Phoebastria nigripes*	N.W. Hawaiian Islands, mostly Midway Atoll & Laysan	47,000	decreasing	2.1m
Laysan albatross	*Phoebastria immutabilis*	N.W. Hawaiian Islands, mostly Midway Atoll & Laysan	590,000	decreasing	2.0m
MOLLYMAWKS					
Black-browed albatross	*Thalassarche melanophris*	Southern Ocean islands, mostly near S America	600,000	decreasing	2.4m
Campbell albatross	*Thalassarche impavida*	Campbell Island, south of New Zealand	21,000	increasing	2.4m
Shy albatross	*Thalassarche cauta*	Islands near Tasmania, Australia	12,500	not known	2.6m
White-capped albatross	*Thalassarche steadi*	Islands south of New Zealand, esp Disappointment Island	75,000	stable	2.6m
Chatham albatross	*Thalassarche eremita*	Chatham Islands	5,300	stable	2.2m
Salvin's albatross	*Thalassarche salvini*	Mostly on the Bounty Islands, New Zealand	31,000	poss declining	2.5m
Grey-headed albatross	*Thalassarche chrysostoma*	Sub-antarctic islands in the Atlantic, Indian & Pacific oceans	95,000	decreasing	2.2m
Atlantic yellow-nosed albatross	*Thalassarche chlororhynchos*	SE Atlantic islands, esp Gough, Tristan & Nightingale	27,000-40,000	declining	2.0m
Indian yellow-nosed albatross	*Thalassarche carteri*	Indian Ocean islands, esp Amsterdam, Prince Edward & Crozet	32,000	declining	2.0m
Buller's albatross	*Thalassarche bulleri*	Snares & Solander Islands, New Zealand	14,000	increasing	2.1m
Pacific albatross	*Thalassarche platei*	Chatham Islands	17,000	stable	2.1m
SOOTY ALBATROSSES					
Sooty albatross	*Phoebetria fusca*	S Atlantic & S Indian Ocean islands, esp Gough & Tristan	13,300	declining	2.0m
Light-mantled (sooty) albatross	*Phoebetria palpebrata*	Circumpolar sub-Antarctic, 35°-78°S latitudes	20,000	not known	2.2m

Recommended Reading

W L N Tickell, *Albatrosses*, Pica Press, 2000.

Michael Brooke, *Albatrosses and petrels across the World*, Oxford University Press, Oxford UK, 2004.

John Warham, *The Petrels*, Academic Press, 1990.

John Warham, *The behaviour, population biology and physiology of the petrels*, Academic Press, 1996.

Useful Information

Save the Albatross campaign (Birdlife International): **www.birdlife.org/seabirds/save-the-albatross**

The Agreement on the Conservation of Albatrosses and Petrels (ACAP): **www.acap.aq**

General information on albatrosses – Wikipedia: **www.en.wikipedia.org/wiki/albatross**

Index

*Entries in **bold** indicate pictures*

Biographical Note

Tony Martin's interest in seabirds began in the Shetland Islands (where he saw his first albatross as an undergraduate), and then happily co-existed with his career as a marine mammal researcher, principally in the polar regions. Formerly with the Sea Mammal Research Unit and British Antarctic Survey, Tony is now Professor of Animal Conservation at the University of Dundee. He also directs the South Georgia Habitat Restoration Project for the South Georgia Heritage Trust.